FADE IN:

EXT. UPSTATE NEW YORK - DAWN

Heavy fog, foreboding hills.

INT. GYM - DAY

                    MAXWELL
          Six...seven...*come on—*

SEALS strains under a stack of weights.

                    MAXWELL (CONT'D)
          ...nine...ten!

Seals sits up and exhales, surveying a room of muscular men.

INT. GYM - DAY

Seals and Maxwell walk past old weightlifting equipment.
Alpha males stand around, as if in a prison yard.

EXT. PARKING LOT - DAY

                    SEALS
          I have a message from T.J.—

He makes a call.

                    SEALS (CONT'D)
          Harrison isn't with us...just me
          and Maxwell...

Yelling comes through the phone.

                    SEALS (CONT'D)
          I heard that he was sick and
          hospitalized.

Seals ends the call.

                    MAXWELL
          What are you talking about,
          Harrison will be closing with us.

                    SEALS
          I was just fucking with him.

They step into a car and speed off.

INT. MALL - DAY

Seals and Maxwell walk through a decaying shopping mall.

INT. STORE - DAY

                    HARRISON
          Hey!

Harrison is dressed in a tight Oxford shirt with an open
collar. Seals and Maxwell are still in gym clothes.

                    SEALS
          I'm going to change—

He walks to the back of the store, where shelf after shelf of
inventory is kept.

INT. BATHROOM - DAY

Seals fastens a thick leather belt, as a toilet flushes, and
then walks out of the bathroom.

INT. HALLWAY - DAY

T.J., an enraged old man, lunges and shoves Seals into
shelves of shoeboxes.

                    T.J.
          *Why did you tell me that Harrison
          is sick*!

He punches Seals in the face.

                    SEALS
          I was joking!

                    T.J.
          He's like a son to me!

T.J. keeps hitting. Tears run down Seals' face.

                    SEALS
          I'm sorry—

T.J. holds Seals against a shelf, pushing his face into boxes
of shoes.

                    T.J.
          I was terrified that something had
          happened to him!

Seals falls to the ground, crying.

                    SEALS
               (whimpers)
          I'm sorry—

                    T.J.
          Get the fuck out of my store.
          You're fired.

                                        DISSOLVE TO:

EXT. STREET - DUSK

Maxwell and RIPLEY, in open-collared shirts and blue blazers,
walk through a silent downtown.

                    MAXWELL
          Are there buyers?

                    RIPLEY
          There might be a few—

                    MAXWELL
          So when do we show my photography?

                    RIPLEY
          Tomorrow evening, during the street
          festival.

INT. LOST DOG CAFE - NIGHT

Red lights illuminate a room, as dated dance music plays.
Seals' well-groomed face is scuffed.

                    HARRISON
          A girl in Pennsylvania, I wanted to
          marry her—

                    SEALS
          What happened?

                    HARRISON
          I left to come up here and she kept
          the ring. I guess I still have a
          fiancée...

They laugh.

                    SEALS
              (to a BARTENDER)
        I'll take the Radical with crema
        and cocoa—

                    HARRISON
        Do you think that Maxwell's work
        will sell?

                    SEALS
        In this town?

INT. LOST DOG CAFE - CONTINUOUS

An older man appears:

                    KRAMNICK
        Harrison—

                    HARRISON
        Hey!

                    KRAMNICK
        Did you lock up my building?

                    HARRISON
        Yeah. This is Seals—

They shake hands.

                    HARRISON (CONT'D)
              (to Seals)
        Things might be changing. Who's
        with Maxwell?

They look across the bar at Maxwell and two young women, one
of whom is ruthlessly attractive.

EXT. STREET - NIGHT

Patrons pour out of bars as closing time nears; a train
rumbles in the distance.

EXT. STREET - CONTINUOUS

The air is dank from a nearby river.

                    SEALS
        I need to split and meet Ripley.

                    HARRISON
          I hope you come back to work—

Seals smiles.

                    SEALS
          We'll discuss that later.

                    LANA
          Bye!

The gorgeous girl waves seductively, as she crosses the
street with Maxwell and an entourage.

                    SEALS
               (under his breath)
          Fuck—

                                             CUT TO:

EXT. LONG ALLEYWAY - NIGHT

Ripley and Seals walk in silence. Sodium lamps are overhead.

EXT. LONG ALLEYWAY - CONTINUOUS

                    RIPLEY
          Where should we go?

                    SEALS
          Millennium, before they close.

They emerge beneath an ornate, red brick building onto a
foggy street.

                    RIPLEY
          My parents sent me to rehab in this
          building—

EXT. STREET - NIGHT

Seals and Ripley walk through an abandoned commercial
district: boarded-up storefronts and nobody around.

                    SEALS
          What's the story with Maxwell?

                    RIPLEY
          His photography show?

                    SEALS
      Yeah.

                    RIPLEY
      It feels like it could do well—

                    SEALS
      ...*could attract girls*?

Ripley laughs.

                    RIPLEY
      Surely that crossed the minds of
      those others.

                    SEALS
      Which?

                    RIPLEY
      Kramnick is a real predator—

                    SEALS
      How so?

                    RIPLEY
      That's what his setup, his
      building, is about: a lure.

                    SEALS
      I've heard that he's a piece of
      shit.

                    RIPLEY
      From who?

                    SEALS
      Harrison.

                    RIPLEY
      Yeah. He has enemies.

INT. MILLENNIUM CLUB - NIGHT

Dour music plays.

                    SEALS
      What do you have?

                    RIPLEY
      Just Oxy—

                    SEALS
      Damn, nothing up?

                    RIPLEY
          This is it.

                    SEALS
          Let me grab some—

Ripley hands him pills, which they down with vodka.

                    RIPLEY
          You know the only good thing about
          these?

                    SEALS
          What's that?

                    RIPLEY
          They work.

INT. MALL - MORNING

Skylights and sunlight.

INT. STORE - DAY

Maxwell uses a corded phone behind a cash register.

                    MAXWELL
          What time should I drop off my
          photos?

His shirt is unbuttoned to nearly halfway down his chest.

                    MAXWELL (CONT'D)
          Will you do a private opening
          before?

A droning voice comes through.

                    MAXWELL (CONT'D)
          Perfect. I'll see you this
          afternoon!

EXT. STREET - DAY

Kramnick sits outside of a restaurant. A vintage Hasselblad
camera is on a tripod next to him.

                    WAITRESS
          Sake?

She sets a bottle and small cup on the table.

                    KRAMNICK
          By chance, have you modeled?

                    WAITRESS
          I have not—

                    KRAMNICK
          You'd be perfect for a project that
          I'm working on.

She blushes.

                    KRAMNICK (CONT'D)
          Let me give you my card. I'd love
          to offer a studio tour—

INT. GYM - DAY

Seals stresses under a shoulder press.

                    SEALS
            Spot me!

Harrison supports his elbows.

                    SEALS (CONT'D)
          ...*eleven*...twelve.

INT. GYM - CONTINUOUS

                    HARRISON
          What did you think of that girl
          last night?

                    SEALS
          Impeccable. Who is she?

                    HARRISON
          Her name is Lana. She lives out in
          the country, but might drive in for
          Maxwell's show—

Seals unwraps a protein bar.

                    SEALS
            A diamond.

INT. GALLERY - DAY

Ripley stands on a stool, painting a wall white.

                    MAXWELL
          Ripley—

Maxwell steps into an unlit art gallery.

                    RIPLEY
          How do you feel?

                    MAXWELL
          Confident!

                    RIPLEY
          Is that your van outside?

                    MAXWELL
          Yeah, I rented it.

                    RIPLEY
          Let's unload your work—

They walk through the cavernous gallery and out into
sunlight.

EXT. MALL - DAY

The mall's cracked concrete exterior looks like an earthquake
struck.

                    HARRISON
          You coming back to work after your
          scuffle with T.J.?

                    SEALS
          Why would I?

                    HARRISON
          What choice do you have?

                    SEALS
          I might apply to the call center,
          or get out of town—

                    HARRISON
          Where will you go?

                    SEALS
          Maybe the City, work in the fashion
          industry.

Harrison smirks.

                    HARRISON
          How could you pull that off?

                    SEALS
          I can't.

                    HARRISON
          People pretend that things are
          fine; it's been a taboo depression
          for years—

                    SEALS
          There aren't options above minimum
          wage.

                    HARRISON
          Speaking of which, I'm heading into
          work.

INT. GALLERY - DAY

Maxwell and Ripley mount portrait photographs.

                    MAXWELL
          Who did you invite to the opening?

                    RIPLEY
          Some from the university, others
          from banks and law firms.

                    MAXWELL
          That sounds excellent!

                    RIPLEY
          I wouldn't get too optimistic; they
          love to stop by and socialize, but
          rarely buy.

                    MAXWELL
          When do they arrive?

                    RIPLEY
          Around seven.

EXT. STREET - DAY

Seals rolls up in an aged sedan and parks. He walks along a
cracked sidewalk, past a restaurant.

                    SEALS
          Yo!

Kramnick looks up, as if confronted.

11.

                         SEALS (CONT'D)
              You have that building downtown?

                         KRAMNICK
              I do—

                         SEALS
              Is that a Hasselblad?

EXT. STREET - CONTINUOUS

From behind, Lana interjects:

                         LANA
                   What's up?

She carries a water pitcher.

                         SEALS
                   Killing time before Maxwell's show—

Kramnick is frigid, not liking what he sees.

                         LANA
                   I'll see you there!

She looks down at Kramnick:

                         LANA (CONT'D)
                   More water?

He gazes at Seals with icy eyes, then back to Lana, and
laughs.

                         KRAMNICK
                   You've got to get this guy out of
                   here.

Seals smiles as if it were in jest. After bitter silence, he
walks away.

                                        DISSOLVE TO:

EXT. GALLERY - DUSK

Maxwell and Ripley watch the street fill with people for a
festival.

                         MAXWELL
                   It looks like we'll have a crowd—

                    RIPLEY
          Your private opening begins
          momentarily.

                    MAXWELL
          Is there anything else you need?

                    RIPLEY
          Just a fistful of Molly—

INT. THE SHOP CAFE - NIGHT

Seals savors a glass of Riesling.

                    LANA
          Hi—

He turns, surprised to hear her voice.

                    SEALS
          Did you just get off work?

                    LANA
          I did.

                    SEALS
          Let me get you a drink—

INT. GALLERY - NIGHT

Maxwell's show is bustling.

                    RIPLEY
          Maxwell, this is Doctor Gorgrant, a
          trustee of Cornell University.

They graciously shake hands and are photographed.

INT. BAR - NIGHT

Kramnick sits and orders whiskey. He surveils the crowd for
young women. A juiced-up BOUNCER stares at him like a jackal.

INT. GALLERY - NIGHT

Maxwell shakes hands in a crowd.

INT. THE SHOP CAFE - NIGHT

Seals puts his hand on Lana's leg; her eyes open wide. She
swirls a glass of rosé:

                    LANA
               (whispers)
          Yes.

INT. BAR - NIGHT

Kramnick stands, vain and erect. The bouncer whispers with
another muscular man.

INT. BAR - CONTINUOUS

Suddenly, the bouncer charges and swings savagely at
Kramnick, pummeling him to the ground.

INT. BAR - CONTINUOUS

Kramnick's mouth drips blood, eyes shut.

                                        FADE TO BLACK.

EXT. BARREN HIGHWAY - MORNING

Serene sunbeams.

EXT. SKYLARK DINER - DAY

Seals walks to his car. He hasn't slept.

INT. GUTTED FACTORY - DAY

Maxwell steps into a freight elevator. Its doors close.

INT./EXT. BARREN HIGHWAY - DAY

Seals drives with blaring music.

INT. STUDIO - DAY

Elevator doors open. Maxwell steps out, into his studio, with
soaring windows.

INT. STUDIO - CONTINUOUS

Ripley turns:

                    RIPLEY
          It was a bust—

                    MAXWELL
          It was packed!

                    RIPLEY
          Yeah, with no buyers.

EXT. MALL - DAY

Seals' sedan pulls up.

INT. MALL - CONTINUOUS

Seals strolls through commercial catacombs.

INT. STORE - DAY

                    HARRISON
          You coming back to work?

                    SEALS
          I'm catching a Greyhound bus to New
          York City.

                    HARRISON
          When?

                    SEALS
          Today.

INT. STUDIO - DAY

                    MAXWELL
          I'd still call it a success.

                    RIPLEY
          It wasn't.

                    MAXWELL
          Why!

                    RIPLEY
          I was banking on this to make my
          budget. I'm underwater—

                    MAXWELL
          What does that mean?

                    RIPLEY
          It means that was the last show.

INT. STORE - DAY

T.J. emerges from the back hallway.

                    T.J.
          Back for work?

                    SEALS
          Fuck you.

                    T.J.
          Shall I call the police?

                    SEALS
          Fuck the police.

                                        CUT TO:

INT. WHOLE IN THE WALL CAFE - DUSK

The restaurant is all reclaimed wood; a man plays piano. Lana
sits and orders papaya.

INT. WHOLE IN THE WALL CAFE - NIGHT

Seals pushes open a thick wooden door.

                    SEALS
          Have you been waiting long?

                    LANA
          Only a moment.

                    SEALS
          So what's the plan?

                    LANA
          I'm taking a Greyhound out of town.

                    SEALS
          To where?

                    LANA
          Maybe Allentown—

                    SEALS
          To do what?

                    LANA
          Maybe escort. Just to get out of
          here—

                    SEALS
          So what the hell is left?

                    LANA
          I think it's over.

They exit to bleak and empty streets.

INT. MOTEL - MORNING

An old radiator hisses.

INT. MOTEL - DAY

Seals answers his phone:

                    SEALS
          Yeah?

                    HARRISON (O.S.)
          You split?

                    SEALS
          To survive—

                    HARRISON (O.S.)
          Do you know that Ripley overdosed?

                                        CUT TO BLACK

●

●